Confidence With Women – How To Approach and Talk With Women

DR HITEN VYAS

CONTENTS

ACKNOWLEDGMENTS

I would like to acknowledge you the reader, for your desire to overcome your fear of women and live the life you want.

I also express gratitude to Dr Bobby Bodenhamer and Dr L. Michael Hall for providing the source of the belief changing techniques included in this book.

HOW TO USE THIS BOOK

This particular book is about helping men overcome the fear of women and helping them to improve the first part of the dating process from a man's perspective, which is approaching and getting into conversations with women.

In order to get the most out of this book, it is best to read it in chronological order. Reading Chapter 1 will give you an introduction about the fear of women you may have and highlights the general approach this book will take to help you overcome this fear.

Chapter 2 will look at negative beliefs you may have about women and Chapter 3 outlines how such beliefs are created in the first place. Chapter 4 is an important one as it contains a very powerful technique you can use to replace negative beliefs you currently have about women, so that you completely change your self-image when it comes to women.

Chapter 5 also contains an empowering exercise you can use to install new and powerful beliefs about yourself and women into your life and take steps to start interacting with women with confidence. Chapter 6 delves deeper into how you can use eye contact and take cues from a women's body language so that you can approach ladies with a calm self-assuredness.

Chapter 7 shows you the essentials of good conversation so that you will never be stuck for anything to say when you talk with women. Chapter 8 gives you advice on the best types of clothes to wear before you meet women.

Chapter 9 teaches you another formidable technique to blow out excuses that hold you back from getting out and meeting women.
Are you ready to turbocharge your confidence with women?

If so, let's get onto Chapter 1!

1 INTRODUCTION

The fear of women

As a guy, talking to women might be something you find hard. The difficulty usually comes from worry. Underlying this worry is fear you will be rejected by a girl you like. You may believe you're not good enough for a particular girl to like you.

This worry might have to do with your low self-esteem or low self-confidence. All of these stem from the beliefs you currently hold about yourself and women.

Overcoming this fear

In this book, you will learn powerful techniques that are focused around overcoming limiting and negative beliefs you have about yourself and women. The techniques will allow you to break old beliefs down, change their meanings and replace them with more confidence and optimism. In the next chapter, we will take a look at some old beliefs about interacting with women which you may currently have.

2 NEGATIVE BELIEFS ABOUT WOMEN

At present you may have a number of negative beliefs about women. Some of these might be like the following:

"I can't talk with girls because I never know what to say to them."

"I'm shy around girls."

"Girls wouldn't like me because I'm weird."

"I'm not good enough."

"I'm not rich enough."

"I'm not tall enough."

"I'm too fat."

"I'm too thin."

"I'm the wrong colour."

"I'm too ugly."

"I don't hang out in the right social circles."

"I'm not clever enough."

Such beliefs usually have a structure to how they are created. You will learn more about this is in the next chapter.

3 HOW BELIEFS ARE CREATED

In this chapter you are going to learn the basics about beliefs in order to understand how you create beliefs about women like those covered in Chapter 2.

We can have beliefs in many things. For example we may have political beliefs and believe in the policies of a certain party.

People may also have religious or spiritual beliefs.

Our most, strongest beliefs are developed during childhood and are passed down from families.

We also have many beliefs about ourselves.

Beliefs about ourselves are developed through our life experiences.

Such beliefs about ourselves are very powerful and can determine what we can do.

And what we cannot do.

For example, if a person really believes they can do the Tango, then they will have the motivation to learn how to dance.

On the other hand, if a person believes they can't stop smoking then the chances that they will not are higher.

We can also develop a number of negative and limiting beliefs about women which may hold us back. Let's take an example.

This is Rajeev, who is getting ready to go out. He is single and has a fear of women.

He is getting ready to meet some friends in a bar for some drinks.

Rajeev is looking forward to it, but also expects girls to be out and feels depressed when he thinks about how he can't go up to them talk with them.

As he is getting ready he begins to have automatic thoughts in his mind such as "I can't walk up to a girl and say "Hi". "I will not know what to say if girls join us". He thinks "I will be shy and girls will think that I'm weird".

Such thoughts lead Rajeev to experience a lot of fear and anxiety.

Rajeev ends up sending a text message to one of his friends to let them know he can't make it.

Rajeev ends up staying at home alone.

So how are beliefs formed?

Well a belief is formed as a result of thoughts that have been repeated over and over again until they have been confirmed as true.

Beliefs can be thought of as ideas, concepts, and ways of living- attitudes that we have said "Yes" to and have let inside of ourselves.

The question then is "Can beliefs which we have allowed inside of us, and said a big 'Yes' to, be changed?"

The answer is yes. How can we do this? Instead of saying "Yes" to limiting beliefs we can now say a Big "No" to them.

And say a big "Yes" to beliefs that empower us.

Say for example that a person has a limiting belief that they can never do public speaking.

The person can learn to say "No" to this limiting belief.

And say "Yes", to being able to speak confidently.

In the same way you can say "No" to limiting beliefs about women and "Yes" to empowering beliefs about women.

The next chapter teaches you exactly how to do this.

4 CHANGING BELIEFS ABOUT WOMEN

In this chapter, you are going to learn a very useful, practical and powerful technique to remove old and unhelpful beliefs about yourself and women and replace them with more positive and empowering beliefs. Have a pen and piece of paper handy to make a few notes and be in a room where you won't be disturbed.

Step 1: Pick an old, unhelpful belief when it comes to women that you don't want.

Think of an old belief that you currently have about women and would like to remove. It could be for example, "I lack confidence and can't talk with women" or "That girl in my biology course wouldn't date me because I'm not good looking enough," or any other belief about women that limits you.

Take a few minutes to think of one and then write it down.

Step 2: Pick a new, empowering belief that you do want.

Now what type of empowering belief about women would you like to have in place of the limiting one? It could be for example "I am a confident person and I can talk to women," or "I can ask that girl in my biology class out on a date," or any other empowering belief about women that you would like to welcome in your life.

Take a few minutes or so to think of one and then write it down.

Step 3: Get a good strong No!

In the third step, think of something that with every part of your body you can say a big "No!" to, fully and completely.

For example, would you ignore a person while they are asking how you are?

No, you wouldn't, because it's rude.

Say "No!" again, but this time louder. And again. Keep saying "No!" until you notice completely what it is like to say "No!" in such a way. In fact take a snapshot of how it feels when you say "No" with so much conviction.

Step 4: Say "No!" to the limiting belief.

As you continue to feel this powerful "No!" completely, think of that limiting belief about women, and say "No!" to this limiting belief until you begin to feel that it no longer has any power to control the way you think or feel or until there is no room for such a stupid belief in your mind.

For example, if your limiting belief is "That girl in my biology course wouldn't date me because I'm not good looking enough" then you would say "No!" to this belief powerfully.

Also use your hands and body language to gesture and support this powerful "No!"

How many more times with that voice, tonality and gesturing do you need to totally shatter that old belief to pieces? Go ahead and keep saying "No!" as many times as you need.

Step 5: Access a good and strong "Yes!"

Think about something that with all your might you can say "Yes!" to without any question or doubt.

It could be something simple, such as answering a question such as "Do you know what day it is today?"

Notice what your "Yes!" feels like. Notice how your "Yes!" sounds. Gesture with your arms "Yes!" Amplify this "Yes!" even more.

Step 6: Say "Yes!" to the new positive belief.

As you continue to feel this powerful "Yes!" fully, think of that empowering belief about women you thought of earlier and say "Yes!" to this new belief you are bringing into yourself. Keep saying "Yes!" Say it even louder. Keep gesturing "Yes!"

For example, if your empowering belief is "I am a confident person and I can talk to women" then you would keep saying "Yes!" to this belief loudly.

Do you want this? You do? Really? How many more times do you need to say "Yes!" right this moment, in order to feel that you have fully welcomed your new belief into yourself?

Step 7: Look into the future.

Imagine your future living with this belief. Do you really want to keep this? Would this improve your life? Would it be valuable to you?

Step 8: Putting your new belief into practice.

Next, answer the following three questions. Make a note of your answers on a piece of paper.

What one thing can you do today to help reinforce this new empowering belief you have welcomed and installed into yourself today?

What one thing can you do tomorrow to help reinforce this new empowering belief you have welcomed and installed into yourself today?

What one thing can you do the day after that to help reinforce this new empowering belief you have welcomed and installed into yourself today?

For example if the belief you have welcomed into your life is "I am a confident person and I can talk to women," then one thing you could today to express this new belief is to go to a shopping mall and approach three women asking them if they know the directions to a particular store. One thing you could do tomorrow is to go to a bar with your friends in the evening and walk up to a woman you like and introduce yourself. The day after that you could go to your local supermarket and start a conversation with the cute girl who works there.

Step 9: Do the three things you wrote in Step 8.

In this step, do the three things you said you would to help reinforce the new empowering belief about yourself and women you have welcomed into your mind-body.

Step 10: Saying "No!" to three more unhelpful beliefs and "Yes!" to three more empowering ones

After you have done your three things from Step 9, repeat Steps 1-9 for three more unhelpful beliefs you currently have about women.

5 HOW TO CREATE BELIEFS THAT BECOME A PART OF YOU

The technique in the above chapter is a very powerful one. It allows you to begin to overcome limiting beliefs you have about women and replace them with new and empowering ones.

In this chapter, you will learn another equally effective technique to really support and internalise powerful ideas about women that you will bring into your life so they become a part of your very fibre.

The steps in this technique are as below. Have a pen and piece of paper handy to make notes.

Step 1: Identify an empowering principle or concept about women that you would like to incorporate into your mind-body.

This principle or concept would be an understanding that you want to set as a way of being in the world when it comes to women.

For example, your principle or concept could be that you want to be confident in your interaction with women.

Whatever principle or concept you choose, it needs to compelling and clear and be able to put into the statement, "**I understand…**"

Use some examples below to help you. I would encourage you to use your words and use the following as a guide.

"**I understand** I am confident in my interaction with women."

"**I understand** I will talk to women with assertiveness."

"**I understand** I will ask that girl in my genetics class out on a date."

Once you have thought of your own principle and understanding, write it down, finishing off the sentence, "I understand…" After you have done this say it out aloud using a powerful tonality.

Step 2: Describe the Principle as a Belief.

In this step you will describe the principle or concept you stated as an understanding in Step 1 as a belief.

Before you do, first contemplate for a moment what life would be like for you if you really believed your understanding.

Now state the concept as a belief saying **"I believe…"**

For example if your understanding from Step 1 above was "**I understand** I am confident in my interaction with women." Now you would put this as a belief by stating the following: "**I believe** I am confident in my interaction with women."

For your own understanding, now state is as a belief firstly by writing it down. After you have written it down, say it out aloud using a strong voice and empowering tone.

As you say it out aloud, just notice how it makes you feel.

Step 3: Describe the Belief as a Decision.

In order to now make the belief into something, which is action orientated, you will describe the belief you stated in Step 2 as a decision by finishing the sentence, "**From this day forward…**"

For example, if your belief statement from Step 2 was "**I believe** I am confident in my interaction with women," then for this you would describe this by completing the following sentence, "**From this day forward**, I will be confident in my interaction with women."

Step 4: Rephrase the Belief and Decision as an emotional way of being.

In this step you will rephrase the belief and decision again and notice what it would feel like if you fully believed it.

For a moment, consider what you would be feeling if you fully believed this empowering belief and decision and living it?

Just allow yourself to experience the emotions you would if you really believed this belief and decision and allow those emotions to grow and expand. As the feelings grow, just imagine there is a volume dial inside your centre and turn the dial so that you emotions grow even stronger.

Next, put your feelings into words by completing the sentence "**I feel...**"

For instance, if your belief from Step 2 was "I believe I am confident in my interaction with women," and your decision from Step 3 was "From this day forward, I will be confident in my interaction with women," then in this step you would state this through the feelings this belief and decision creates in you, such as **"I feel** confident and assertive. **I feel** relaxed and playful and am ready to enjoy myself."

For your own belief and decision, put your feelings into words by writing and completing the sentence "I feel..."

Step 5: Turn the emotions into actions to express the belief and decision in the real world.

In this step it is time to create some actions you can take in the real world so that the belief and decision truly become a reality for you.

In order to do this, write down and complete the following sentences:

The one thing I will do today as an expression of this belief and decision and its corresponding feelings is to...

And the one thing I will do tomorrow as an expression of this belief and decision and its corresponding feelings is to...

And the one thing I will do the day after that as an expression of this belief and decision and its corresponding feelings is to...

For example, if you wrote "I feel confident and relaxed." as an expression of the belief statement, "I believe I am confident in my interaction with women," and your decision statement, "From this day forward, I will be confident in my interaction with women," then you might complete the following sentences:

The one thing I will do today as an expression of this belief and decision and its corresponding feelings is to give that girl I like a call and ask her out on a date.

And the one thing I will do tomorrow as an expression of this belief and decision and its corresponding feelings is to walk up to that girl I like who works at the department store and start a conversation with her.

And the one thing I will do the day after that is to walk up to a girl I like when I'm in a bar, say "Hi" to her and ask her how her how her night is going?

So, for you own feelings you wrote in Step 4 for your particular belief and decision, now complete the following, first saying each out aloud and then writing it down on a piece of paper:

The one thing I will do today as an expression of this belief and decision and its corresponding feelings is to...

And the one thing I will do tomorrow as an expression of this belief and decision and its corresponding feelings is to...

And the one thing I will do the day after that as an expression of this belief and decision and its corresponding feelings is to...

Step 6: Complete Steps 1-5 for three more principles and concepts about women you would like to incorporate into your mind-body.

After you have completed Steps 1 5, including the three actions you will take in Step 5, do Steps 1-5 again for three more powerful principles and concepts about yourself and women you would like to make a part of you.

6 USING BODY LANGUAGE TO YOUR ADVANTAGE

The previous two chapters were all about reorganising your belief system about women. By completing these chapters properly, you should have some real powerful and juicy beliefs about yourself and women going around in your mind-body.

This chapter will now show you how you can use your own body language and the signals women give off to you, to really understand which women like you and want you to go over and talk with them so that you maximise your chances of success.

The power of eye contact

One thing which guys are afraid of the most when it comes to interacting with women, which even stops them from making an initial approach, is believing the girls they like will reject them.

There is one powerful part of your body you have at your disposal, which you can use to really know whether that girl you're looking at likes you back.

It is through eye contact.

Women look at things they like. If they see things they don't like, they don't look at them. They do the same thing with guys. If they like you, then they will look at you. If they're not interested then they won't look at you.

The way you use eye contact is through the following:

You look at the girl you like in the eyes and try and get eye contact. You do this in a soft way. Do not stare as this is creepy!

You then see if the girl you're looking at looks back at you directly in the eyes. If she does, and she locks eyes with you for 2-3 seconds, then this is a very good sign. If she looks at you for about a second, looks away then doesn't look at you again, then it is likely she isn't interested.

If she does hold eye contact with you for 2-3 seconds then step right over and introduce yourself!

If she smiles while making eye contact then this is a big green light! Proceed to walk over and say "Hello."

Also, a lot of guys make the mistake of focusing so much on a girl who doesn't find them attractive. By doing this they fail to look around at other attractive girls who would give them eye contact only if the guy made the effort to look in the first place!

If you're out with your friends and see a girl you're interested in, see if you get some eye contact. If she's not looking at you, then don't waste your time. Take a walk around the environment you're in and find girls who are interested in you.

Exercise

As an exercise to practice eye contact, when you are out with your friends in a bar or at a restaurant, just look around at women who interest you and see who looks back into your eyes for 2-3 seconds. Those who do most likely think you're cute!

Glancing your way is a good sign!

Another way you can tell if a girl likes you is if she keeps glancing your way. For instance, she might be talking with some friends and then casually turns her head to look at you and then quickly look away. If she does this 2 or 3 times, then this is a good chance she is interested. Get over there quickly!

She won't tell you to and come and talk with her!

In an ideal world the girl who is giving you eye contact would just yell over to you to come and have a chat with her.

Unfortunately, reality isn't like this. Girls won't do this. They too have a fear of being rejected. Hence they use eye contact and soft glances as ways of expressing their interest in you.

Guys, as men you need to use your eye contact and other body language clues like glances which girls give you as a sign to go over and start a conversation.

Standing near you is a good sign as well

Another good sign a girl is interested in you is if she comes and stands close by to you. If you're standing in a bar or some type of party, and if you have noticed a girl checking you out from a distance, and suddenly she ends up close by to you with her friends then this another signal that she is interested. Use it to boldly walk up to her and say "Hi."

Check your own posture

Also, when you do walk up to a woman you like, ensure your posture is correct. By correct posture, you need to be standing upright, with shoulders back slightly, with your head up so that you look confident and it will make you feel confident too.

7 CONVERSATION

Initial words

An area which many guys find hard is what to say when they initially approach a women they like. The initial words that come out of your mouth really don't have to be difficult. Just avoid using any cheesy 'pick up' type lines.

A simple "Hello" is all it takes. Or something like "Hello, I saw you from over there (point to where you were standing) and I wanted to come over and meet you." has worked wonders for me personally.

Ask her about her

Another stumbling block guy's face when it comes to making conversation with women is worrying they won't know what to say, or that they will run out of things to say, so won't be able to continue with a conversation.

There is one thing you have at your advantage, which can make conversation very simple for you. It is this. Women love to talk! And they love to talk about themselves.

So in order to get women to talk about themselves, you need to take an active interest in them and ask them questions about themselves. Every so often you can interject with an "Ok, that's interesting," or "Ok, so tell me some more about that."

By asking questions about the women you are interacting with, you will have already differentiated yourself from most of the guys out there who just talk about themselves and show off about their money and cars, which usually comes across to women as being insecure and is a quick way to bore them and put them to sleep!

Open ended questions are the best

When you talk with women, it's always best to ask open ended questions beginning with "What...", "How..." and "When...". These types of questions work great because they allow the woman you're talking with to continue talking.

On the other hand closed ended questions like "Did you..." or "Are you..." usually require either a "yes" or "no" answer and usually are a sure fire way to end a conversation.

Topics to talk about

In order to initiate a conversation there are a number of topics you can talk about. Usually if you are meeting a woman for the first time, a great topic to focus on is the current environment you are both in. It makes sense to do this. You're both meeting for the first time is a certain place. Talking about this environment is a good way to start a conversation.

For instance, if you meet a woman in a bookstore then you can ask her about what types of books she likes to read. If you meet a girl in a bar where music is playing then you can make a comment about the current music being played and ask her what types of music she likes.

A technique I personally use when talking with women I've just met is to take one topic and ask open ended questions around this one topic before moving onto another one. What this does is makes you different because most guys don't have such deep conversations and you will seem interesting to the girl you are talking with. Other topics which you can ask open ended questions about when you talk with a woman are:

The types of foods she likes to eat.

What she likes to drink.

Where she has travelled to and where she would like to go to.

What work she does.

Her family.

What her aspirations for the future are.

8 SOME POINTS ABOUT CLOTHES

The main point of this book is to enable you to break down limiting beliefs about women and develop new ones you can use to increase your confidence and your ability to interact with women. However, in order to increase your chances of attracting women when you're out and about it is important that you dress the best as you can. I'm not talking about going out and buying really expensive clothes unless you can afford to. I mean dressing in decent looking clothes that fit your physique well.

Even if you are out shopping during the daytime, you can still wear casual looking clothes that look decent. In the evenings, smart clothes are best. A smart jacket, clean shirt, a good pair of trousers and clean shoes usually work great. Checkout pictures of men in Men's magazines like GQ, FHM and Men's Health to see what guys are wearing to get an idea of what looks good.

9 HOW TO DESTROY THOSE EXCUSES

So far, from reading this book, you've created some powerful and empowering beliefs about yourself and women, and have actually been getting out and interacting with women with a new sense of confidence and empowerment.

However, when you're creating any type of change, which will improve your life, you will come across stumbling blocks.

A common stumbling block when it comes to interacting with women is excuses. For instance, you might be having a drink in a bar and the girl sitting at the table next to you is looking at you. However, you dismiss it as her looking at someone else so that you don't have to get up and say "Hi." Another example would be your knowing you would have the opportunity to meet women on a night out with your friends and then cancelling because you wanted to stay in and watch a TV program instead. Or perhaps you tell yourself you're too tired.

These are excuses, which at the time may seem harmless. However, the more excuses you make, the less you will be actually out meeting women and improving the way you interact with them.

If you catch yourself coming up with an excuse which results in you avoiding talking with women, then follow the following powerful steps to blow the excuse into oblivion.

Step 1: Determine the desired goal.

In the first step, think of something about interacting with women that you would like to do, or that you know would be good for you if you did it.

For instance, perhaps you think it would be good for you to go into a shopping mall once a week, go into some clothes shops and talk with some of the female sales assistants about clothes and get their opinions on what would look good on you.

Whatever your outcome is, just allow yourself to imagine doing it. Do this as vividly as you can so that you can sense what it feels like to have achieved this goal.

Step 2: Let the excuses emerge.

When you think of going ahead and doing your particular action, consider the excuses that come to your mind that stop you from taking action. Consider the ideas, reasons and explanations you use to excuse yourself.

For instance, if your goal is to go into a shopping mall once a week, walk into some clothes shops and talk with some of the female sales assistants about clothes and get their opinions on what would look good on you, then excuses you might come up with are you would rather stay at home and watch the cricket match on TV. Or perhaps an excuse you use might be that it is raining so you can't go outside.

Whatever your excuses are, let them emerge, notice what they are and notice what they feel like.

Next write them down.

Step 3: Analyse the excuse(s).

In this step consider the following questions:

Do you need this excuse or these excuses?

Is there any part of the excuse that has a positive purpose for you? If so, then you may want to preserve this part.

For instance, if your excuse was to stay at home and watch the cricket match, then a positive purpose of doing this is to protect you from the possibility of getting rejected if you are out and meet a girl.

Think of what the positive intention of your excuse could be and then write it down.

Do this for each of your excuses.

Step 4: Preserve what is important about the excuse(s).

Go inside yourself and take out the good aspect of the excuse which serves a positive intention for you and preserve it. Really notice the meaning of the importance of this part of the excuse and suck it out of the excuse so that the excuse becomes a shell. As you extract the important part of the excuse, just notice what it is like as you hold on to this important part separately from the useless excuse.

Check within you to ensure the excuse is now just an empty shell. If it still isn't, keep sucking out the important part so that the excuse becomes a shell.

For example, if the positive intention of your excuse was to protect you from rejection and your excuse was staying at home and watching the cricket match on TV then you might go inside yourself and really focus on sucking out the protection part from the overall excuse of staying in and watching the cricket match. You would do this until the excuse becomes a shell.

Do this for each of your excuses.

Troubleshooting – how to preserve the important aspect of the excuse(s)

If you are wondering how you go inside yourself to search for any positive intention in the excuse then you can do this through the following: Quietly ask yourself what is positive inside the excuse and just notice any images, feelings and sounds that emerge in your mind and body.

Just notice what the excuse means to you. Perhaps you can represent the excuse as an image, or a word or a feeling, or a sound. Whatever way you represent your excuse, use this representation to really suck out the positive intention. For instance if you represent an excuse as an image, then you might suck out the positive intention and represent this as a separate image.

Step 5: Reject the empty shell of the old useless excuse(s).

In this step, access a strong "NO!" state. Expand and amplify this refusal and rejection so that you feel it very strongly. Feel this powerful "NO!" in your body and in your hands and feet. When this sense of "NO!" is at its strongest, imagine the empty excuse in front of you and step into that excuse with the "NO!" state and stomp on it with the strength of your "NO!".

For example, for your empty excuse shell, you would first access a strong "NO!" You could do this by considering something you would never do like eat insects and say "NO!" to eating insects. You would notice the tonality and volume of the "NO!" and you would then notice what this "NO!" feels like. You would then imagine your excuse in front of you and say "NO!" to it, rejecting and refusing it powerfully.

Do this for each of your excuses.

Step 6: Test.

In this step imagine the activity you would like to do, which you know is good for you and notice what happens as you think about moving towards it. What do you feel? What comes to your mind? Test to see whether there are any more excuses lurking that you might use to hold yourself back.
If any other excuses do emerge, take each one through Step 3-Step 5.

Step 7: Make an executive decision to take action

In this step, tell yourself you will do your desired action at the highest level of your mind. You will allow it to become a part of you so that when you think of this activity, you will take action and how you will do it will become a matter of discovery.

10 FINAL THOUGHTS FROM THE AUTHOR

You have reached the end of this book. You have learnt how to completely transform your beliefs about yourself and women so that you can approach ladies with confidence. You've also learnt how you can use body language and especially eye contact to maximise your chances of successfully approaching women.

You also learnt how to converse with women so that you can engage them and really learn about them. You now also have a great excuse busting tool at your disposal, which you can use so that you remain motivated to improve your ability to approach and communicate with women

Once you start to interact with women, it is like learning a new skill. Experiment and try things out. Make a note of what worked well when you approach and talk with women and also record what didn't work so that you are always improving.

Most importantly, please be patient with yourself and don't beat yourself up if you make mistakes. Old ways of thinking about your ability to approach and interact with women can take some time to change. However, the time spent learning, practicing and developing your skills will be well worth it in the end.

I would be delighted to answer any questions you may have about the book or even get some feedback from you. Please feel free to e-mail me at hiten@hitenvyas.com

Now, go and get the girl you want with confidence!

11 OTHER BOOKS BY THE AUTHOR

How To Overcome Job Interview Anxiety.

Hoe To Cold Call With Confidence.

How To Present With Confidence.

Mindfulness Meditation For Everyone.

Say No To Exam Stress.

12 BIBLIOGRAPY

Dilts, R., 1999. Sleight of Mouth: The Magic of Conversational Belief Change. Capitola, CA: Meta Publications.

Hall, L.M. and Bodenhamer, B.G., 1997. Mindlines: Lines for Changing Minds. Clifton, CO: Neuro-Semantics Publications.

Wright, J.H., Basco, M.R. and Thase, M.E., 2006. Learning Cognitive-Behavior Therapy: An Illustrated Guide. Washington DC: American Psychiatric Publishing, Inc.

13 ABOUT THE AUTHOR

Dr Hiten Vyas is the founder of Stuttering Hub Limited
(http://hitenvyas.com), a company specialising in providing coaching
services for people facing communication challenges. As a life coach, he is
passionate about helping people increase their self-confidence and
overcome fears related to communicating.

Hiten is based in Leicester in the UK and is available for private one-on-
one consultation locally. He is available internationally and in India through
telephone coaching. He is a Neuro-Linguistic Programming (NLP) Master
Practitioner and uses NLP-based techniques in his coaching practice.

He has personally overcome some of his own deepest fears to lead a
successful life. He has reached a position where he now believes that a
person can achieve all they want in life, no matter how they communicate.
He loves and embraces change. He is passionate about helping other people
change and live fulfilled lives.

Hiten also has a PhD in Biomedical Information Systems from
Loughborough University in the UK.